I0420531

Psychological Advantage

Master the Art of Psychology –

Make a Difference Helping People with Emotional Problems

Thomas Abreu

Table of Contents

All rights reserved. No part of this publication may be reproduced in any form without written consent of the author and the publisher. The information contained in this book may not be stored in a retrieval system, or transmitted in any form by any means, electronic, mechanical, photocopying or otherwise without the written consent of the publisher. This book may not be resold, hired out or otherwise disposed by way of trade in any form of binding or cover other than that in which it is published, without the written consent of the publisher. Respective authors own all copyrights not held by the publisher. The presentation of the information is without contract or any type of guarantee assurance. All trademarks and brands within this book are for clarifying purposes only and are the owned by the owners themselves, not affiliated with this document.

Disclaimer
The information contained in this book is strictly
for educational purpose only. The content of this
book is the sole expression and opinion of its
author and not necessarily that of the publisher. It
is not intended to cure, treat, and diagnose any
kind of disease or medical condition. It is sold with
the understanding that the publisher is not
rendering any type of medical, psychological,
legal, or any other kind of professional advice. You
should seek the services of a competent
professional before applying concepts in this book.
Neither the publisher nor the individual author(s)
shall be liable for any physical, psychological,
emotional, financial, or commercial damages,
directly or indirectly by the use of this material,
which is provided "as is", and without warranties.
Therefore, if you wish to apply ideas contained in
this book, you are taking full responsibility for your
actions.

Introduction

"A person whose behavior pushes you away is a person that needs connection before anything else." It is true, when someone is going through a tough time in their life, they need to feel some form of connection – they need to know that there is someone in this world that loves and cares for them. Sometimes, simply sitting down and talking to the individual will be enough, while other times, you'll need to dig deep in order to be able to help the one in front of you.

Normal people just like you can master the art of psychology and help those that are dealing with emotional troubles. By emotional trouble, we are talking about PTSD, depression, stress, anxiety and various other forms of psychological trauma. For years, I worked alongside people that developed psychological trauma and was available to reach out to them and give them a helping hand.

Today, I would like to introduce you to my book titled "Psychological Advantage: Master the Art of Psychology." I wrote this book because I care about helping others and I would like to share my knowledge with you so you may help yourself and help others as well.

1: What Is Psychology?

Defining Psychology

I'm sure most of us have our own preconceived notions of what psychology is and what it is all about, but for now I would like you to throw everything out the window and start from scratch. Okay? Let's begin.

Psychology Isn't Just About Therapy

Remember, psychology is not just about therapy. When individuals think of psychology, they have a tendency to picture a therapist sitting in a comfortable room with a notepad as he/she writes down ideas as their client talks about their childhood experiences. Therapy is a big part of psychology, but that's not all there is to it. In all actuality, there are many psychologists that don't work in the field of mental health. Psychology has other areas, including research, teaching and consulting and they work in a wide variety of settings such as:

- Private corporations
- Colleges
- Universities
- K-12 Schools
- Government offices
- Hospitals

Let's start off with understanding the actual word, "psychology" and break it down into its fundamental parts …

The word itself is made up of two Greek words: *psyche* which means "breath, spirit, soul or mind" and *logos* which means "study or knowledge". So, by combining those two words together, you end up with most direct and simplest definition of psychology - "the study of the mind."

Of course, as you may already know, there are more detailed and comprehensive definitions out there. According to the British Psychological Society, "Psychology is the scientific study of people, the mind and behavior. It is both a thriving academic discipline and a vital professional practice" and according to the American Psychological Association (APA), it is "the scientific study of the behavior of individuals and their mental processes."

With all of this in mind, we get a pretty good idea of what psychology is about: It is the scientific study of how a person's mind works and how he/she behaves. But even though this definition seems easy and understandable, the actual study itself is far more complex. That is because the mind is complex!

The mind is so intricate that even to this day; we

have yet to have a full understanding of it. There is so much left for us to learn about how people think, reason, feel, remember, dream, and perceive things that it seems that we might never truly understand it at all!

However, I think it is best that we start by understanding what psychology is not and in the next section, we will delve into that a little bit more.

Psychology ≠ Psychiatry (Psychology is NOT Psychiatry)

A very common misconception about psychology is that it is the same thing with psychiatry. It is not! The two words are not interchangeable. As we have already defined, psychology is the study of the mind while *psychiatry* is a more in-depth discipline which mainly pertains to the study and research of mental disorders and illnesses.

Also note that, in the case of psychiatry, it is a medical degree and only doctors can practice psychiatry legally. Psychology on the other hand focuses on much broader areas and not only in mental problems, though there is also a branch(s) of psychology that deal with that as well.

Branches of Psychology

Now, speaking of branches of psychology, in this

section we will be discussing several of them very briefly:

1. *Abnormal Psychology*

This is a branch of psychology that pertains to the study of abnormal behavior as well as psychopathology. It is particularly focused on researching and treating an array of mental disorders such as in psychotherapy. It is also very much connected to other branches of psychology such as clinical psychology which we will discuss later on.

2. *Biological Psychology*

Biological psychology, also known as biopsychology, is the study of how biological processes can influence a person's mind and his or her behavior. This branch of psychology goes hand-in-hand with other areas of science like neuroscience and uses medical tools such MRI and PET scans to look at the brain when trauma happens such as when there are brain injuries or abnormalities.

3. *Clinical Psychology*

In this area or branch of psychology, it is focused more on three things: (1) the assessment, (2) the diagnosis, and (3) the treatment of mental disorders. It utilizes scientific theories in order to further understand as well as predict and/or relieve people of a certain mental disability that maybe discomforting them or hindering them from functioning properly in daily life. Over the years, this branch of psychology has become much needed especially because of its use of psychotherapy.

4. Cognitive Psychology

The research largely done here is meant to understand how humans tick. It tries to investigate how people not only think but also communicate with one another, perceive the things around them, their memories, as well as their ability to learn. There is so much involved in this particular branch of psychology, therefore, it is very much interlinked with many other disciplines such as neuroscience, philosophy and even linguistics.

5. Comparative Psychology

In this branch, comparative psychology is concerned with studying animal behavior in hopes of getting a better understanding on the human psyche. If we know more about how other living things think (meaning animals), we might get a better understanding of ourselves as well.

6. Developmental Psychology

This area focuses more on how humans develop and the growth over their entire lifespan. This does not only pertain to early childhood development, but goes on through a person's adolescent years and very much into their adult lives. It includes everything and anything psychological in a person's life such as motor skills, problem solving, morals, language, emotions, personality, the concept of self as well as self-identity. Like most other branches of psychology, it overlaps with other branches of psychology as well as other disciplines in the hopes of further understanding the very complex living organism, the human being.

7. Evolutionary Psychology

Evolutionary psychology takes a deeper look into human behavior throughout its evolutionary lifespan. The main theory of evolutionary psychologists is that psychological factors such as memory perception and language are very much products of natural selection. They believe that all our human psychological traits are mere products of adaptations that our ancestors learned in order to survive during their time.

8. Forensic Psychology

This applied branch of psychology solely focuses in using psychological research and principles in criminal investigation as well as law. A forensic psychologist therefore practices his knowledge of psychology within the criminal justice system and civil courts. They also must have a good understanding of criminal law because they are very much involved with other members of the criminal justice system - lawyers, judges, etc. Usually, a forensic psychologist's role in these situations is to testify in court and present to the jury psychological findings that pertain to a case.

9. Industrial-Organizational Psychology

This is also an applied branch of psychology that uses psychological research in order to increase people's (usually a company's) work performance, as well as help in the selection of employees, improve product designs, and enhance usability within a company.

10. Health Psychology

Health psychology or also known as behavioral medicine or medical psychology, is the branch of psychology that was established in order to observe how the combination of behavior, biology and social context influence illness and health in general.

This means, while a medical doctor is trying to treat an illness, a health psychologist could be trying to figure out how the illness even occurred through his investigation of the patient's socio-economic status and background that could have influenced their behaviors which could impact their treatment of the disease.

11. Neuropsychology

This is the branch of psychology that centers on the study of physical structure of the brain and its function in relation to certain and specific human behaviors and psychological processes. It is also involved in the recording of electrical activity done on higher primates such as chimpanzees and apes that help us understand human brains as well.

12. Occupational Psychology

This is the same as industrial-organization psychology or work psychology. An occupational psychologist's aim is to increase effectiveness, efficiency and overall satisfaction in the workplace.

13. Personality Psychology

This branch takes a look at the various elements that make up a certain individual and that individual's personality. This includes such theories as:

- Freud's structural model of personality
- "Big Five" theory of personality

14. School Psychology

In school psychology, as the title implies, its main focus is using psychology within the educational system and give assistance to children with emotional, social, and even academic issues that need addressing in order to create the best educational experience available to them.

15. Social Psychology

This branch of psychology uses scientific methods in order to study three social factors:

- Social perception
- Social influence
- Social interaction

This means that it pretty much delves into people's group behavior, their social perception, leadership, nonverbal behavior, conformity, aggression and even prejudice.

As you can see, the study of the mind isn't as simple or straightforward and has many different areas that need addressing. In the next section below, I will be mentioning a few of the most popular schools of thought that were developed by some of the famous psychologists of the past.

Schools of Thought

1. Structuralism

Considered the first school of thought in psychology and formally established by one of Wilhelm Wundt's (the father of psychology) more prominent students, Edward B. Titchener. This school of thought focused on the breaking down of mental processes into its most basic components through the use of introspection.

2. Functionalism

In reaction to the first school of thought, structuralism, functionalism was formed by a man named William James and was very much heavily influenced by the evolutionary theory of a certain Charles Darwin. Functionalists, unlike Structuralists, focus on the purpose of the consciousness and behavior as well as the individual's differences.

3. Psychoanalysis

Founded famously by Sigmund Freud, this school of thought is focused on how the unconscious mind influenced a person's behavior. He was the individual that originally discovered that the mind was composed of three elements which we have come to know as the id, the ego, and the superego. Surely, you are familiar with those three elements.

4. Behaviorism

Founded by John B. Watson, behaviorism was the school of thought that believed that behaviors could be measured, trained and therefore changed over time.

5. Humanism

This particular school of thought came about during the 1950s and was a response to the domination and maybe overuse of psychoanalysis and behaviorism during the time. It was the belief of humanists that psychoanalysists and behaviorists were too pessimistic in their way of thinking. Humanists on the other hand, were more optimistic in their views in that they focused more on each person's individual potential and would rather stress on the importance of a person's growth and self-actualization.

6. Cognitivism

This is probably the youngest school of thought out of all that are mentioned here. However, it has since become a very popular branch of psychology in its own right. The focus in cognitivism is such topics as thinking, decision-making, problem solving, learning, attention, memories, forgetting, and even language acquisition.

What is psychology like now? Well, psychology is definitely still very much used today as is seen by all the applied branches mentioned above.

However, unlike before, there hasn't been a major movement since the mid-1900s, and therefore, psychology has become more eclectic in the sense that it has mixed and matched the best of each of the doctrines from the aforementioned schools of thought.

Many psychologists use these principles and methods as therapists in order to help other people who have certain mental, behavioral and emotional disorders.

However, psychologists aren't the only ones using psychological methods. Teachers for example use many methods developed by psychologists to help them create the best learning environment for their students. Psychology is definitely something that is always going to be used. The "mind" is something that "we humans" need to understand so it will never go unstudied.

2: The Origins of Psychology

Okay, so now that you have read chapter one and have a full understanding of what psychology is, in this chapter, I would like to explain the originals of psychology.

What is "psychology"?

Let me remind you - Psychology is considered an academic and applied scientific study of the mind and behavior. It is applied to various aspects of human life like work, family, and in some cases, even in the treating of mental health problems.

Early Forms of Psychology: Philosophy and Physiology

Unlike other sciences, psychology is a relatively new scientific field with the bulk of its advances only having happened in the 19th century. However, it does have its beginnings far back in the 4th or 5th centuries in philosophy from several ancient civilizations like Greece, Egypt, China and India. Psychology was, for the most part (up to the middle of the 19th century anyway), only a branch of philosophy before it was finally developed and made into its own scientific discipline.

During this time, philosophers such as Socrates, Plato and Aristotle, were able to identify "seat of the mind," the brain and even went as far as to speculate how it worked and its functions. They also explored abstract concepts such as pleasure, pain, motivation, rationality, knowledge, and mental illness that are all still being discussed and pondered on to this very day.

Sometime during the Medieval Period, psychology (still considered as philosophy at this point) developed a little more. Muslim philosopher, Ahmed ibn Sahl al-Balkhi was one of the very few who first suggested that the mind had a tendency to get sick and that the body may manifest it as a physical illness. This was later to be commonly known around the world as "depression."

It was also during this time that other conditions were emerging such as:

- Hallucination
- Mania
- Dreams/Nightmares
- Epilepsy
- Paralysis
- Stroke
- Vertigo

There were also advances in therapeutic treatments to such ailments (mentioned above) though they were not labeled as such back then as psychotherapy and music therapy.

Then it was during the Enlightenment Period in the 17th century that we had more contributions from philosophers such as Rene Descartes, Thomas Hobbes and John Locke. Their contributions and in-depth analyses of the nature of the mind and soul were the basis of clinical psychology as a discipline of modern medicine.

Dualism vs. Monism

Speaking of Rene Descartes, he was a French man who came up with the concept of "dualism." He theorized that there was a separation between the body and the mind. According to his theory, the body's behavior was scientifically measurable because it was the physical side of a person while the mind was the spiritual side that could not be measured. Descartes surmised that the only way the two sides were connected and interacted with one another was through the pineal gland.

On the other side of the pond, two Englishmen named Thomas Hobbes and John Locke totally rejected Descartes idea of dualism. It was their belief that the mind and body are one and the same. This was later to be called "monism." It is their theory and not Descartes' that most psychologists continue to believe in and much research has gone into supporting it.

It has been shown through many researches that

indeed, the physical and mental aspects of human beings are not in fact separated but closely interconnected. It is from this basis that the fields of psychoneuroimmunology and behavioral medicine focus on to this day.

Debunked Psychological Developments

It should be noted that despite psychology steadily becoming more of a legitimate scientific study by the time the 17th century rolled in, it wasn't totally devoid of some false theories here and there.

One such theory was called "mesmerism" (later and more commonly known as "hypnotism") named after a man named Franz Anton Mesmer. Mesmer theorized that every human being was a "fluid" that could be controlled by the gravitational forces of the earth and that this controlling of the "fluid" inside a human could help cure diseases. He would then test his idea on a patient who reportedly got better after this method was done on her and Mesmer and "mesmerism" became very popular throughout the Victorian era and even to some extent (in the form of hypnosis and hypnotherapy) today.

However, Mesmer's theory was later investigated and found to be nothing more than a false treatment and the findings of the investigation were published, making Mesmer instantly unpopular. He was exiled out of Paris and was never heard from again.

Another study was "phrenology" or the study of the brain as well as the structure of the skull in order to establish personality traits and the mental disposition of a person. This idea was developed by another man named Franz, Franz Joseph Gall and it too became widely popular during the 19th century just like mesmerism. And like mesmerism, it was later regarded as obsolete.

Despite no longer considered as true sciences, mesmerism and phrenology do have some influence on modern day psychology as they both placed some of the ground work of what will be neuropsychology and psychiatry. Therefore, they should be given a brief mention in this article as well.

Scientific Revolution: The Advent of Experimental Psychology

A certain Johann Friedrich Herbart was said to be among the very first to come up with a way to make a more scientific psychology in which you would do away with most pseudoscience. In order to do so he was attempting to apply mathematics in order to measure external stimuli and the resulting sensations.

There were other people - Bessel and Donders to name a few - also began mathematics to measure certain things like reaction time and mental speed. But it was not until Wilhelm Wundt came around did psychology finally have its founding father.

Wilhelm Wundt, Father of Psychology

It was in Leipzig, Germany that Wundt founded the very first laboratory dedicated solely to psychology and its research. He was the first person to actually call himself a psychologist and he was the author of the very first textbook on psychology - *Principles of Physiology and Psychology*.

It was he who believed that there was a need to study the conscious thoughts of human beings and that that was the key to unlocking the mind. His work was groundbreaking in the sense that he was basically laying the foundation of what will be our modern psychological experimentation.

Despite future criticisms of his process known as introspection as being unreliable and unscientific, and its lack of objectivity, it is still easily one of the greatest achievements made in psychology to date and still an approach used in modern neuroscience research even to this day. Therefore, with this in mind, his impact in psychology is without a doubt of great importance.

Structuralism - Psychology's First School of Thought

It was one of Wundt's students (and one of the famous ones at that), Edward B. Titchener, who, expanding on Wundt's own ideas, found the theory of structuralism.

This theory was an attempt to figure out and understand the mind, focusing on three things in particular:

- Individual elements of consciousness
- Organization of these elements into complex experiences
- Correlation of these mental phenomena with physical events

It was he who placed strict guidelines when using introspection. However, despite this, structuralism was also heavily criticized because of its reliance on introspective analysis and its unreliability. According to critics, it was impossible to get feasible results because the self-analysis introspection, more often than not, yielded different results depending on the person or subject.

From Structuralism to Functionalism

Because of such criticisms, structuralism began to struggle in its survival to be a legitimate scientific method and therefore, newer and better approaches in psychology began to pop up. One of these was functionalism. Founded by William James in the late 19th century, functionalism, based structuralism's concern for the anatomy of the mind, was the precursor to what we now know as behaviorism.

Behaviorism

James was far more interested in the way the mind was able to adapt depending on the person's environment and the situation that person was in. Functionalism, as was mentioned above, would later influence other psychologists to create theories on human behavior and that is how behaviorism came about.

Behaviorism was a widely popular theory back in the 20th century in the United States. Based directly from psychoanalysis (Sigmund Freud), behaviorism was more focused on a person's issues such as:

- Self-identity
- Death
- Aloneness
- Freedom
- Meaning

Behaviorism changed the game in the psychology

world. It tried to detach itself from former ideas of the conscious and unconscious mind, focusing solely on observable behavior instead.

Ivan Pavlov, Russian physiologist, had the earliest record work on behaviorism. It was his research on dogs and their digestive systems that he stumbled upon what is known today as classical conditioning which was very much a big deal during the time it was founded.

Thus, the impact of behaviorism continued and it was of particular influence for the next fifty years or so. It was another behaviorist after Pavlov that furthered the theory of behaviorism. His name was B.F. Skinner and it was he who came up with the concept of operant conditioning which showed the effects of reinforcement as well as punishment on a person's behavior.

However, like its predecessors, behaviorism too lost its status in field of psychology. Yet, we continue to see its influence even to this day. Classrooms all around the world continues to use these basic principles to help students to learn and cope better in school.

Other contributions to behaviorism that are still very much used today are:

- Maslow's Hierarchy of Needs

- Carl Rogers' client-centered therapy

Cognitivism - The Rejection of Introspection

Another psychological school of thought was cognitivism. While accepting the use of scientific methods, it rejected introspection, psychoanalysis and it acknowledged that there existed internal mental states which behaviorism did not. Cognitive psychology today is continuing to advance and with the help of technology has been able to make strides in the understanding of how the brain and neural systems work.

Psychology, though relatively new has gone through some major advancement and developments over the years. Modern psychology applies all of the theories and methods mentioned above in order to find better ways to help people - especially those that suffer from mental problems.

Through the use of psychoanalytical therapy combined with behavioral theories, humanist concepts, and cognitive understanding, psychologists can figure out the human mind and provide the best possible solutions.

Of course, this doesn't mean that newer and better things are no longer found in today's psychology. As mentioned before, technology has opened doors for newer developments (as well as more questions) in the field. Much has yet to be explored when it comes to the human mind and not everything can be explained quite yet.

In fact, there are far more unanswered questions still awaiting psychologists, but hopefully through more research in genetics, doctors as well as psychologists will get a better understanding of the human mind. And there have been some significant discoveries of late. New genes that relate to behavior and personality were found and they are a welcome challenge for psychologists for sure.

With these new discoveries and through some bioengineering and other technologically-advanced techniques, it is possible to create medicines and even cures that will help people that suffer from neuropsychological symptoms.

Our society today has become more susceptible to things such as depression and eating disorders, not to mention a rise in people with special needs. All of these aspects could not be managed or understood well enough without psychology and therefore, it is definitely very much in demand today. But while further advancements in psychology are yet to come, for now, psychologists can continue to rely on old and trusted theories from the beginning of the field.

3: How Can Psychology Help People?

If psychology wasn't as important as it is today, I wouldn't have even bothered to write this e-book for people to read. I am fully focused on reaching out and helping people, which is why I chose to share my knowledge on psychology. In this chapter, I am going to tell you how psychology can be used in order to help people, so pay close attention to what I have to tell you here …

First of all, let me ask you this – do you know how psychology can help people? Do you realize how useful psychology is when it comes to the human mind?

Psychology is a hot button issue among the nation today as it is used and often borrowed from many other fields of study, culture, and life. However, on the same note, there are many that feel as if psychology is overpowering our lives, and defining us before we have a chance to define ourselves.

Look at it this way, we justify murdered by saying that their childhood trauma erased the chance for a normal childhood, and thus negatively affected their adult lives. We use psychology to understand the minds of cult followers, and to understand everyone around us. It feels as if we are constantly being scrutinized, out faults being laid bare by the mass that is psychology.

However, we should not see it as such a negative entity. We need to stop viewing it as something that is negative, because it is quite the opposite. It is here for the betterment and understanding of humanity.

Psychology is the study of the human mind, including how it works, and why we react the way we do to given situations and contexts. We are not trying to justify the murderer, but at the same time, we are trying to understand how we can prevent that from happening again. By understanding our brains, learning the secret codes that make us who we are, we can better understand the world around us.

Psychology helps people deal with trauma and fear

In a perfect world, nobody would need to deal with the drama that is dealt out by devastating events such as war, assault, and the death of family and loved ones. But this is not a perfect world and people often need help in recovering from these traumas, which is understandable.

When a person is deeply wounded emotionally, often times, they aren't able to find their way out on their own and will require some form of help from another human being. Depression, anxiety, phobias, and anger can often present themselves as symptoms of this emotional damage.

Just as you go to the doctor when you break a bone or injure yourself, you should go to the psychologist and turn to someone else when you receive emotional wounds. Psychology knows the pathways of trauma, and when you feel like there's no way out of the your trauma you have created, psychology can set you up on the right track.

Without this aid, many people would find themselves trapped within their own misery and suffering, unable to find a way out. Psychology can be a guide to the human mind and its intricacies, saving people from unnecessary pain.

Helping children through the trials of growing up

Growing up can be a tough, trying times for even the most well adjusted child. Everyone faces unfortunate events that they have to face through their childhood whether it is bullying in any form, parents who have gone through a divorce, and socialization issues while growing up during school years.

Bullying and cyberbullying is a nationwide epidemic that too many kids have to live with everyday. It can destroy confidence, and lead to anxiety and depression.

Psychology has the tools to help children through the bullying and gives them the knowledge to resolve the situation in the future. Parents may try to help their child during these lonely and scary moments in their lives, but it may not always work.

Many children have problems fitting in with their peers for a variety of reasons, whether its anxiety, an attention disorder, or fear. By properly diagnosing and treating these symptoms, children will have a much better chance at making friends and socializing with their peers.

Helping children get through Divorce

Divorcing parents can often tear a child's world apart, making them feel alone and isolated. During this time, children may feel overwhelmed, whether they are toddlers or teenagers. Psychology can help reach out to children/teenagers and prepare them for the long road that is ahead of them.

Unfortunately, in this day and age, one out of every two marriage ends up in divorce. Parents who are getting a divorce tend to worry about the effect it will have on their children. During this hard period, parents may be preoccupied with problems of their own, but they will still continue to be the most important people in their children's lives.

Parents may be relieved by the divorce, but the

children may be confused and frightened, because there is a threat of their security. Parents may feel so upset about the divorce, that they turn to the child for direction or comfort, which can add even more stress to the child.

Sometimes, children believe they have caused the divorce and some even take on the responsibility of getting their parents back together, which causes them additional stress.

Unless parents tell them what is happening, divorce can be misinterpreted by children. Regardless, divorce sets the child up to vulnerability to both mental and physical illnesses due to the traumatic loss of a parent through divorce. With psychology, however, a family's strengths can be mobilized during the divorce.

Speed up recovery from a brain injury

Every year, around 1.7 million people in the United States alone sustain a traumatic brain injury. Of those people, over 270,000 are hospitalized and unfortunately, at least 50,000 die. Yes, traumatic brain injury happens for a variety of reasons, but it generally shows up after acute damage to the brain from things such as a stroke, infection, tumor, or head injury.

There are so many cases of traumatic brain injury,

but the three most common ones include firearms, car accidents and falls. There are various types of traumatic brain injuries that exist and can cause lasting damage to the individuals, along with their families.

The first type of injury is called a mild traumatic brain injury. This is defined by disorientation, confusion, memory loss, irritability, fatigue and loss of consciousness for less than thirty minutes. This injury is often referred to as a concussion.

The second type is called severe traumatic brain injury. This will involve a loss of consciousness for over thirty minutes. This injury may result in language impairments, cognitive deficits or seizers.

Psychology can help individuals that have received a brain injury speed up the recovery.

Helping the justice system perform to the best of its ability

As we learn more about the human mind and how it reacts to certain events and situations, we can use this information to better improve our criminal justice system.

As we learn more about mental health issues, we can better address and punish those who engage in criminal activity because they did not know any better. We can also better train our police officers to handle every situation that can arise, without necessary risks on either side.

Our judges and lawyers understand why the human mind makes certain connections and how those connections can inform actions. Mental health awareness does not excuse criminal behaviors, but by understanding how the two are correlated, we can better protect ourselves and our society, and prevent it from happening again.

Improve our overall mental health

Mental health is a stigma that does not easily shed itself, and psychology works to change that. Whether mental illness is bad or not does not matter to the millions of people suffering every day. Psychology wants to help these people and improve their lives.

This can take on many forms, whether it is helping a woman with post partum depression after the birth of her child, or a war veteran with posttraumatic stress disorder, or a schizophrenic. Psychology does not want to leave anyone behind and it makes great strives to understand these diseases and to better understand how to treat them.

There is no jurisdiction to psychology, it can take itself into any country in the world, any school, any prison, anywhere people inhabit. Psychology will be there trying to understand and treat mental illnesses.

Psychology is crucial to improving our mental health

Psychology is a helpful and necessary tool in order to protect and safeguard our communities, whether that is shown through helping a child through a parents' divorce, helping an assault victim, or simply listening to the problems of others. It is a helping hand that can lift you up when you need it the most and tell you that you are not alone. If we can better understand our minds, and thus ourselves, we can better understand the world around us.

Here is a look at some more things that psychology can help you with …

Adds Motivation

Whether your goal is to lose weight, learn a new language or quit smoking, psychology can be used for motivation. In order for you to increase your motivational levels when approaching these tasks, try these tips:

- Set clear goals that are related to the task
- Vary the sequence to prevent you from getting bored
- Introduce new elements to keep you

interested
- Give yourself a reward for a job well done

Help You Get Better at Communication

Communication goes deeper than speaking and writing. Nonverbal communication will make up a large portion of your interpersonal communication. In order to be able to get your point across effectively, it is important that you learn how to express yourself nonverbally and read the nonverbal signs of those in the room. Here are some strategies to follow:

- Notice nonverbal cues in others
- Make eye contact
- Learn how to use the proper tone of voice in order to reinforce your message

Help Your Leadership Skills

Regardless of the task, whether you are a volunteer or an officer, having good leadership skills will help you in various points of your life. Mind you, not everyone is born a leader; this is something that will take time to develop. However, according to my psychological research, there are various ways you can improve those leadership skills. Here are some ways:

- Talk about possible solutions to problems

within the group
- Offer guidance, but give group members the opportunity to state their opinions
- Focus on stimulating ideas
- Reward creativity

Helps You Understand Others

Yes, psychology can also help you understand others. Having the ability to understand other human's emotions will play an important role in your professional life and relationships. Emotional intelligence is a term that is given when talking about the ability to understand not only your emotions, but also the emotions of other people. So, what can you do in order to become more emotionally intelligent? Here are some strategies for you:

- Record your emotions and experience on paper
- Look at situations from the perspective of another individual
- Assess your emotional reactions

Helps You Make Accurate Decisions

During my years of research on cognitive psychology, I learned that it can help individuals make more accurate decisions. By taking these strategies and applying them to your own life, you will be able to learn to make wiser choices. The next time you need to make a major decision, try these techniques:

- Look over the potential benefits of the decision
- Look over the potential costs of the decision
- Look at the situation from various viewing points, including emotional, rational, negative, positive, intuitive and creative perspectives.

Do Better in School

Research has showed us that taking tests can actually help an individual better remember what they have learned, even if it wasn't covered on the test. Another study found that taking a test may be a better memory aid than studying. When trying to gain new knowledge, self-test yourself on a frequent basis in order to input what you have learned into your memory.

Be Healthier

Believe it or not, psychology is also a useful tool for improving your health. From ways to better nutrition and encourage exercise to treatment for depression, health psychology has a wide array of beneficial strategies that can help keep you healthy. Here are some things you can do:

- Both artificial light, as well as sunlight, can help reduce the symptoms of seasonal affective disorder.
- Exercise can be a good treatment for depression
- Helping people understand the risks behind their unhealthy behaviors can help them make healthier choices

4: Why Should People Bother to be Happy?

Why does it seem like being happy has become an elusive commodity nowadays? Happiness seems to be such a faraway state of being in a world full of sadness, anxiety, and general negativity. But there is a reason (or rather reasons) why we should all strive for some measure of happiness, and hopefully this book will help you find your happiness.

Okay, so why should people bother to be happy in the first place?

Here are 8 benefits you will receive from focusing on being happy (in no particular order):

Less Stress

Don't we all want to be stress free? I know I sure do. In all honesty, I wish I wasn't such a serial-worrier. People who are trying to be happy have the added advantage of eliminating some, if not all of the negativity in their lives. Their happy and positive approach to life not only helps them but radiates to other people so that not only does that particular person feel happy but he or she makes those around them feel happy and comfortable as well.

The opposite is also said to be true. Don't you absolutely hate that grumpy co-worker who comes in to work with a perpetual scowl on his face and a grumbling attitude every time you have to interact? Those types of people can eliminate the good feeling in a room and add to the stress of a possible stressful situation. So laugh and be merry - the people around will secretly thank you for it, I guarantee it!

Good for Your Health

Another reason to be happy is that it surprisingly adds to your good health! Happiness does equal healthiness. An Irish proverb says, "A good laugh and a long sleep are the best cures in the doctor's book." And there is some truth to that.

Scientific research has proven that people who say that they are generally happy about their lives have lower heart rates, lower levels of cortisol, lower risk to heart disease, and are far less likely to have diabetes, strokes, and depression.

Those who have an optimistic view on life generate more immune-boosting blood cells, according to one study. These immune-boosting blood cells help you fight away common illnesses like the flu. It's not the apple that keeps the doctor away, its happiness!

Better Relationships

Happy people seem to have better social lives, relationships and interactions with other people than those who are not happy. This is because a positive person gives off a good vibe and people are generally drawn to people like that. Nobody really wants to hang around a moody person all the time. A person who is happy with the people around them is more likely to create deep and meaningful bonds with the people he or she loves such as their family and friends.

Boost in Productivity

Happy people are able to create positive thoughts despite stressful or downright negative situations and can come up with equally positive actions. These positive actions boost their productivity levels and increase their confidence. Not only are you less like to be stressed, you create for yourself an environment that is conducive to quality work.

Better Problem Solving Ability

You need to have the right attitude in order to see a solution to every problem you face. When a challenge arrives, with the right attitude, it will be easier to overcome them. You probably already know that having the ability to solve a problem skillfully is important. I'm telling you this, because when you are happy, you will be able to look at the plus side of everything – everything, whether you admit it or not, will have a positive side. There is always a solution to a problem, regardless of what it is. By being happy and searching for the positive, situations will no longer take you over.

Beauty

I probably don't have to tell you this, but the most beautiful people are those who are the happiest. I always say "eyes are windows to the soul." When you look into someone's eyes and see true happiness reflecting, you will see just how beautiful they are. A smile will make you shine on the outside and grow on the inside, so go ahead and smile.

A Sense of Fulfillment

Let me ask you something – wouldn't you like to know what it feels like to be content? Wouldn't you like to know what it feels like to be satisfied? If so, in order to see what it feels like, you will need to be happy.

You will never be content, unless you are truly happy. Let me tell you, there's no other feeling in this world that can fill you up as much as happiness can. Music, spending timed with loved ones, whatever you enjoy doing, will give you true happiness.

Once you experience happiness, you will feel as if everything in your life is perfect. You will be able to look at your life in a whole new light – from a positive perspective.

You will finally be able to look past those imperfections, instead of focusing on the small negative aspects of life. Happiness will allow you to look at the larger picture and see the world for what it really is.

Make Others Happy

I don't know about you, but I love making other people happy. There's this quote by Charlie Chaplin "Life laughs at you when you are unhappy. Life smiles at you when you are happy. But, life salutes you when you make others happy." This is one of my favorite quotes. When you're upset, you'll make others around you upset. If you want to make a difference in not only your life, but other people's lives, be happy. I've noticed feelings are contagious.

When you enjoy yourself, you will be able to spread happiness to others around you. Giving happiness, in my opinion, is a very noble thing to do. This is what gives purpose to my life and improves the quality of my life. It eliminates those social evils and bridges all gaps.

People Love You

If you feel "alone" in this world, you may find it hard to believe, but there really are people that love and care about you. Some people look up to you and you may not even realize it – they look at you as if you are the most important person in your life. Those people want you to be happy. That right there should be your starting point – if you can't find any other reason to be happy, make the people you love your reason. You have people around you that love you unconditionally.

Your Achievements

What have you achieved in life? Surely you have achieved something. Think about it – there's got to be some form of positive achievement that will make you smile. When you're feeling down, think about that achievement, it will make you smile and motivate you for further accomplishments.

Gives Meaning and Purpose

Happy people tend to have a deeper understanding of what they want to do and be in their lives. So, why don't you do something you really love? Find time to go on that dream project or do something relaxing. This will not only give you time to mediate and think about your life but it will give you a true sense of peacefulness and happiness.

Satisfaction

We all know that life in general is not a walk in the park. We are always bogged down with the realities of the everyday nature and sometimes it is very hard to feel satisfied with what is given to us. But people who try to be positive and happy tend to have the best outlook on life and find contentment despite whatever problems or obstacles that they face.

Satisfaction is not attained from material or temporary things but by having a happy outlook and good relationships all around you. Not only you should you try to be happy in order to achieve satisfaction but it will give you a boost on your self-esteem and outlook on your life.

Younger Looks

Don't you just love it when a person is constantly smiling and happy? I do. Those people have "glow" about them that I find very appealing. A smile and happy demeanor definitely seems to shed of years from a person that makeup or other cosmetics can't totally hide.

You not only look younger to other people but being happy means that you actually feel younger too! Don't you wish you can be as carefree as a child? They look like they have so much going for them and they do.

You too can adopt their happy mindset. It doesn't mean that you should act like a child of course, but try to imbibe their happiness in the simplest things. This can be very calming and satisfying if you let it. These feelings can also reduce the amount of stress that you feel and eventually, lessen those stress lines on your face!

Positive Energy

Genuinely, happy people have a positive approach to life and that is the key to having a full and amazing life. Their positive mindset sends signals to the rest of the body, telling them to create more endorphin. Endorphin is the chemical within our body that is essential for a person to be happy.

There are some other things I would like to add to this chapter that I need you to realize …

Long-term happiness all depends on your ability to notice and appreciate the fine details. Right now you could take advantage of that skill. Once you receive everything you have asked for in life, you will still be subject to the highs and lows that come with life.

You must learn to enjoy the little things and if you

haven't learned, your well-being will be at risk. Every time something goes wrong in your life, you may feel unhappy. Instead of being negative, and yes, I know this is hard, try thinking about the things that fill you with the most happiness – listening to music, spending time with your pets, running on the beach, spending time with your family, and so on…

For example, focus on things that will brighten your day. This way, no matter what changes, you will be able to have a variety of pleasures to help you through the tough times.

Every day you wake up, it is a new opportunity to be better person than yesterday. That thought right there can increase your self-esteem levels and create happiness. You see, back in the day, I was obsessed with making everything perfect. If I wasn't the best when it came to something, no matter what it was, I wasn't able to sleep.

Not being perfect at something would keep me up all night and that was a very tough life. When I did become great at something, it just wasn't enough, because there was always room for me to be better. With all of that in my mind, I was continuously disappointed in myself.

Now, instead of looking at things as if they have to be perfect every single time, I look at things I do as opportunities to get better. It's easier when you set an attainable goal, like writing an extra page tomorrow, than to obsess over perfection.

If I was in the same shoes as I was years ago, right now, I would be stressing that I wasn't a world-famous author and that would rip me apart. Today, I am simply happy to reach out to the readers and hope that in some way, shape or form, I am helping them.

Take it from me, go ahead and focus on small improvements and set mini-goals, there is nothing wrong with this. By taking this step, you will naturally move yourself toward bigger dreams and you will respect the way you are doing those things.

The World Needs More Happy People

I honestly believe that this world needs more happy people. Every week it seems we hear about a new tragedy that makes us question society today. We live in a world where there will inevitably be famine, war, destruction, and poverty. Here's the thing – where there is evil, there can be good. I mean, take a bad person and a happy person as an example, the happy person can create a ripple effect that can change the world. So, go ahead, start today - make that change you would like change and choose happiness.

If none of the reasons I gave make you happy, go look in the mirror. What do you see? You will see a living person. No matter how tired, sad, unhappy, or sick you are, you are able to stand there, in front of the mirror and see your reflection. That right there is something you can be grateful for. People we love die unexpectedly on a daily basis.

What would you do if you knew today was your last day on earth? Would you spend it stressing over the things you don't have? The places you couldn't go? The people you can't see? I doubt it. Instead, you would make every effort to spend as much time as possible with family and close friends and let them know how much you love them.

Yes, enjoying the present moment is a habit that is going to take some practice. If you are always putting that happiness off and looking towards tomorrow for happiness, you probably aren't going to find it.

As strange as this may sound right now, having the ability to appreciate those things that are in front of you doesn't have anything to do with what you actually own. Instead, it is more so about how you measure things in your life at any given time.

Whatever you do, you need to find reasons to be happy. Happiness can benefit your future. As previously mentioned, a happy attitude is contagious. It is so much nicer to see a genuinely cheerful person. They are well loved and well respected by the people around him rather than feared or hated. They are far less likely to handle problems in a negative manner because of their positive nature.

All in all, happy people are generally awesome to be around and hopefully, we can all strive to be like them. It would be a wonderful world to live in surely, if we could just make the effort to give an individual a smile each day and pass on the happiness. Let's all strive to be happy!

Avoid Letting Anyone or Anything Destroy Your Happiness

Okay, so once you are happy, it is important that you stay happy. You have to avoid letting anyone or anything bring you down. You must realize that happiness is an inside job. Don't go allowing anyone or anything else to have that much power over your life.

I've noticed it is so easy to let what other people do or say affect our happiness. Then, you have those challenges that are randomly tossed at us - have you noticed that when things aren't going the way they should, it really throws you off? I went through many years of torture because I let those around me and various situations have an effect on the way I felt.

I had people that disappointed me, people who did things they shouldn't have done, and many times it felt as if things in life were never going to fall into place. I remember looking at the mirror and saying to myself "you are never going to be completely happy until you make a change."

However, one day, I reached a point in life where I just couldn't take it anymore. I realized that if I let people continue to control my emotions, I wasn't going to live a very happy life.

Yes, there will be challenges and situations you will need to deal with. We will run into with people that says things they shouldn't. You need to realize that this is how life is – we all go through it.

However, we do not have to let those things have control over the way we feel. If you have been letting people control you and bring you down, then you need to find another method to make your days go by easier. You need to do things differently than what you have been doing.

There's a great quote by Joan Borysenko that really fits this scenario. "Every day brings a choice: to practice stress or to practice peace."

Every moment we have a choice to smile. We have to make that choice over and over until it starts to happen naturally. So starting today, learn to put a smile on your face. When you feel yourself getting upset, remember that nice quote "I could choose peace instead of this."

Every day, as you move forward in life, remind yourself that your mindset should be at the top of the list. Remind yourself that letting people interfere with your happiness isn't worth it.

Of course I understand that we are only human and there may be times we have an initial reaction to what people say, or have done things they shouldn't have done when certain situations come up.

However, don't get too upset. Choose not to throw out any negative reactions. Instead, let it rise to the surface. Don't feed others with negative energy. Give time for that energy to evaporate. Push yourself to stand back and take a look in order to see the bigger picture. You will be able to stop yourself before you have a negative reaction.

If things start to get too complicated, it is okay to unwind – go do something you enjoy doing in order to direct your attention to something else. Walking, meditating, listening to music, playing with your pet, spending time with your friends or reading are some activities you can do in order to put your mind somewhere else.

5: Helping Yourself Help Others

It is common knowledge that if you exercise regularly, eat your fruit and vegetables and avoid smoking, you have a much better chance of living a longer, healthier life. Volunteering in your community and giving to others can strengthen your mental and physical health.

Before I go any further into this chapter, I would like to show you some research that has been conducted over the years.

A Paper by Dr. Suzanne Richards

A paper led by Dr Suzanne Richards at the University of Exeter Medical School reviewed 40 studies from the past 20 years on the link between volunteering and health and provided very interesting results. The article found that volunteering is associated with lower depression, increase well-being and 22% reduction in health related issues. The article is freely available in the open access journal BMC public health.

Different volunteers have different motivations for doing what they do. A person may volunteer because of values, they are volunteering to satisfy personal values or humanitarian concerns and with some people this can include a religious component. Someone may volunteer because of community concern; they volunteer to help a particular community, such as a neighborhood or ethnic group to which they feel attached.

A person can volunteer for esteem enhancement; they are volunteering to feel better about themselves or to escape other pressures. A different person may be volunteering to gain a better understanding of other people, cultures or places. A person may also volunteer for personal development; they are volunteering to challenge themselves, meet new people and make new friends, or further their career.

Why People Help Others

Okay, let's look away from volunteering for a second. So, why does someone help another? Perhaps it is because of egoism. You see, it may be egoistic motives that lead us to helping others in poor circumstances in order to reduce the distress we get from watching those terrible situations. Yes, in other words, this means that sometimes, we help others in order to help ourselves.

Walking Away

So why do people walk away when someone is in need of help? This is a way to reduce distress. Not all negative emotions increase helping – when negative emotions are self-focused, an individual will become blind to the opportunity of helping someone. What this means is that only focused people help others more when they feel bad.

The Empathy-Altruism Model

Have you heard of the empathy-altruism model? This model suggests that an individual is able to experience two different types of emotions when they see someone that is suffering – there's personal distress, such as anxiety, alarm and fear, which leads to egoistic helping. Then, there's empathetic concern, such as compassion, sympathy and tenderness, which leads to altruistic behavior.

Altruism is motivated by a desire to help others. As a result to this, individuals that are altruistic will always help, even when they are fully capable of walking away from the stressful situation. The extent to which individuals empathize with the victim plays a major role in them helping the one that needs help. You see, when we feel more connected to the victim, we are more likely to help. Of course, this doesn't mean that connectedness facilitates helping.

The Definition of Altruism

You can define Altruism as putting other people's needs before your own, whether that is offering your seat to a pregnant woman or making a cup of tea for a work colleague. Evidence suggests that helping others can even be good for mental health and well-being as it can reduce stress as well as improve moods, self-esteem and happiness.

You see, you really don't have to volunteer, unless you really want to. There are many different ways that you can help others in your everyday life. Carrying out deeds doesn't need to consume a vast amount of your time or even cost money – making small changes is all the difference you need.

There are numerous benefits to your mental health and well-being by helping others. Helping others promote physiological changes in the brain associated with happiness. Helping others can also bring a sense of belonging and reduce isolation as being part of a social network. Face-to face activities such as volunteering at a drop-in centre can help reduce loneliness and isolation.

Helping others reduce stress as positive emotions can help reduce stress and boost our immune system. Helping others can also help get rid of negative feelings; negative emotions such as anger, hostility and aggression can have a negative impact on our mind and body. By helping others you can decrease these feelings which in turn will positively impact your health.

Helping others may also help put things in

perspective. Someone who helps another person that is less fortunate than they are can give them a real sense of perspective as it makes them realize how lucky they are. This will help give that person a more positive outlook on anything that is causing them stress.

An act of kindness can improve confidence, control, happiness and optimism. The person receiving the act of kindness will also be influenced to repeat the good deed that they have experienced themselves. Evidence suggests that helping others can last a long time, for the act provides a "kindness bank" of memories that can be drawn upon in the future.

Helping others is a fundamental part of humanity as you bond together when you help a fellow man or woman. In times of great tragedy, stories of those who help others can be inspiring, such as stories of people who have helped their nation recover from national disasters and terrorist attacks. Some people even devote their entire lives to helping others, from firemen who run into burning buildings, to the police force that protects our cities.

Of course helping others isn't just limited to grand gestures or during times of tribulation, I mentioned volunteering earlier and this is an example of this. Helping others can be done every day and contrary to what you may have heard, helping others is not always a selfless act. It is important to understand that helping others can actually help yourself.

The Bystander Effect

Research shows that a person is less likely to offer help to someone in distress if other people are also present. This is known as the bystander effect, meaning the probability that the individual will receive help will decrease based on the amount of people that are present in the area.

Contributing to the bystander effect is diffusion of responsibility. You see, when there is a large crowd in the area and another individual needs help, others are going to feel as if they aren't responsible for offering help. If only a couple of people are present, the responsibility will become evenly distributed among those that are present.

Bystanders that have witnessed an emergency will help if three conditions are met. The three conditions include if they interpret the incident as being a true emergency situation, if they notice the incident and if they assume responsibility for helping the individual.

There are certain circumstances where people are more likely to help someone. For example, if they see others offering help and they are not in a hurry, they will help. If they share similarities to the individual in need of help, a person is also more likely to help.

A person is also likely to help another if they have feelings of guilt running through their body. Further research has indicated that happier people are more likely to help an individual in need of help if they appear to deserve help.

The Social Exchange and Social Responsibility Norm

Have you ever heard of the social exchange? Some social psychologists use this theory in order to explain why people reach out to help others. Some experts argue that people help one another because they want to gain as much as possible, while they lose as little as possible.

Social responsibility norm could also be used in order to explain why an individual will help someone else, regardless of whether doing so is costly.

Reciprocity Norm

Reciprocity Norm is another terminology that is used in order to explain helping behavior. The implicit social rule that says people must help those who have helped them is applied in reciprocity norm.

Acting in Their Own Self Interest

Those individuals that are acting in their own self-interest are known for sometimes helping others as well. However, in different circumstances, people can actually harm themselves when they act in their own self-interest.

The terminology "social trap" is given in this type of situation. A classic example of social trap is global warming. You see, global warming is happening because people are acting in their own self-interest when they purchase fuel-inefficient cars.

A Study Conducted by Michael Norton

Michael Norton is a professor at Harvard Business School. He conducted a study with his colleagues back in 2008. During this study, they found that by reaching out and giving money to another individual that is in need of money, the individual who gave the money will be uplifted more than if they spent it on themselves.

The individuals originally predicted that they would be happier spending it on themselves. In a study conducted by Jorge Moll and colleagues at the National Institutes of Health back in 2006, they found that when individuals donate to charities, it activates certain regions of the brain – the regions that are associated with social connection, pleasure and trust. Scientists also believe that this type of behavior produces endorphins in the brain.

A Study by Doug Oman

Doug Ogman from the University of California, Berkely, conducted a study back in 1999. Believe it or not, a large amount of research is linked to various forms of generosity – the research shows us that generosity brings about better health in people.

During this study, he found that older people that belonged to two organizations were forty four percent less likely to die over a five year period in comparison to those who did not volunteer. Sure, this may sound like a normal study to you, but what is so amazing about it is that they factored in the exercise habits, age and general health. They also factored in the negative health benefits, like smoking.

A Study by Stephen Post

Have you ever read the book "Why Good Things Happen to Good People?" If not, it is well worth the read. Let me tell you a bit about this book – Stephen Post, a professor of preventative medicine at Stony Brook University reported that when individuals give to others who have chronic illnesses, they increase their health benefits.

A Study by Rachel Piferi and Kathleen Lawler

Then you have a study done by Rachel Piferi of John Hopkins University and Kathleen Lawler of the University of Tennessee that was conducted back in 2006. During this study, they discovered that individuals who offer support to others had lower blood pressure in comparison to those that didn't. In return, this suggests a direct physiological benefit to helping others.

A Study by James Fowler and Nicholas Christakis

James Fowler of the University of San Diego, California and Nicholas Christakis of Harvard conducted another study. This study is published in the proceedings of the National Academy of Science. It showed that when an individual behaves in a generous manner, it inspires onlookers to behave generously at different times towards other people. Basically, what the study found is that generosity is contagious.

A Study by Paul Zac

The director of the Centre for Neuroeconomic Studies at Claremont Graduate University, Paul

Zac, discovered that by giving individuals a dose of oxytocin, it will cause them to have more empathy and act more generously towards others. For those of you who don't know, Oxytocin is a hormone that is naturally released during breast feedings and sex. It brings about euphoria, warmth and connections to others.

Helping Others Really Can Help Yourself

Do you see what I'm talking about now? Simply by helping others, you are helping yourself as well. Now that I got all of that research out of the way, I want to give you a list of things you can do in order to help others:

Let me start with one of my favorite quotes by Dalai Lama, "If you want others to be happy, practice compassion. If you want to be happy, practice compassion."

Many times, the trend in our society involves people being separated from one another. Cars, for example, have taken us off the streets, where we used to walk and stop to talk to one another and enjoy a nice chat. We have cubicles in the workplace – those have been taken a bite out of the humanity in working.

Television has taken individuals and planted them in their living rooms instead of being outside with other people. Even movie theaters where many people go has stripped true conversation away because we are simply sitting there staring at the screen.

Of course, I am not against any of these inventions. I personally believe these inventions are amazing … except, maybe the cubicle. What we must guard against would be the propensity of that individuality to have focused our minds on the exclusion of others. Instead of helping others in need, the tendency is to focus on ourselves.

Mind you, I'm not saying every single human being is like this, I am saying that it could happen if we are not careful.

Don't you think it's time to stand up against the greed and selfishness that lives in our modern world and help others? Not tomorrow, not the next day, but today, right now.

Yes, helping another person may be inconvenient, but there are many advantages to it:

- It helps you connect with another individual
- It will make you feel better about yourself
- It will improve the life of another person
- The kindness you give can multiply
- It makes the world a better place to live in

So, go ahead, take a couple of minutes today and

show some kindness towards another human being. It doesn't matter what it is – it can be something small or something big. When you show kindness, ask them to pay it forward. Watch, you will be putting a smile upon someone's face and that in return will make you smile just as big.

If you're not used to helping others, you may not know where to start. Here's a little list that will help you get that thinking cap on:

Volunteer at a Charity

There are so many different places you can volunteer at. For example, if you have a love for animals, call your local animal shelter and see what it takes in order to volunteer there. Volunteering is one of the most amazing things you could do.

Be Friendly Towards Others

Simply smiling and being friendly towards others can go a long way. By smiling, you place a warm feeling in their heart and you may even make their day a little bit better, causing them to reach out and do the same to someone else.

Make a Donation

Surely you have something you don't use. Drop them off to someone who is in need. Seriously, this is a good way to put your clutter to use.

Stop to Help Others

The next time you see someone sitting on the side of the road with a flat tire or someone that is in need of help somehow, stop and ask them if there is anything you can do to help. Sometimes, all they need is a simple push or to use your cell phone in order to call someone they know.

Share Your Knowledge

Take time to share your knowledge with others. This could be as easy (or hard) as teaching your grandmother how to use the computer or teaching someone how to ride a bike.

Offer Comfort

When you see someone who is in need of comforting, go ahead and offer your comfort. Hug them, lend a helping hand, be their listening ear or offer a kind word – doing this will go a long way.

Buy a Homeless Person Some Food

The next time you see a homeless person sitting outside a store, as bad as this may sound, you should avoid giving them cash. Giving cash may be a bad idea, because they could purchase bad things with it. However, what you could do is buy them some food and be friendly to them.

Help Someone Who Needs it

When you see someone who looks as if they are dangling over an edge, talk with them and urge them to get help. If they don't, dial the suicide hotline in order to get advice.

Help Someone Exercise

If you know someone in your life who would like to stay healthy, you could lend them a helping hand. Offer to go walking together or join a fitness program with them.

Send a Nice Email

Give a quick note to someone telling them how much you enjoy having them in your life, how happy you are with them, how proud you are of them, or simply thanking them for something they did.

Just Be There

When an individual appears as if they are in need, sometimes simply being there can go a long way. Sit down with them and talk.

Create a Care Package

Reading material, soup, chocolate …anything you can think of that you believe the person will enjoy, throw it in there.

Share Your Own Resources

Surely you have some resources that you have invested in? Share them with someone else. Perhaps one of your contacts needed help on a quick job? Perhaps you have season tickets to a game you won't be attending? Keep those unused resources in the back of your mind and try to offer them to others who could use them.

Show Someone an Opportunity

I am always keeping an eye out for opportunities knocking on my door. It could be a potential partner or a nice business opportunity. Once an opportunity shows up, think about who you know that could benefit from it. For example, I personally like to help others who have friends or family members who are looking for a job. Many times, I am able to use my own connections in order to find some work for them.

Giving Gifts to Others

Yes, I understand, giving gifts to others can be a bit on the tricky side, because you don't want to appear as if you are "buying" people. You should get an individual a gift that makes sense to them – something that will help them. When a major hurricane hit years ago, I sent care packages to survivors as they recovered from the impact of the hurricane. You see, this type of action could be contagious – people have a tendency to remember who helped them when they needed help.

I understand helping others isn't always easy and it may be a lot of work. It can sometimes throw your schedule out of whack, cost you money and make you to lose time, among many other things. Sometimes, it can even be taken the wrong way.

However, I encourage you to keep these tips in mind and use them from time to time. This way, you'll be able to show your connections that they really are important in your life.

6: 5 Keys to a Positive Personality

When watching television or reading the news today, it can be hard to find positive things, I admit that one – that's how it has always been. Shootings, war, and social divisions splatter across our views, and often, it causes us to feel negatively about ourselves and the world around us.

Let me ask you a question - what if we want to fight these negative thoughts and feelings? What do we do? Mind you, not everyone has a natural positive personality, but there are ways that we can change the way we think, and make ourselves into happier, more positive people.

The benefits of a positive personality are endless, from being happier, more productive, better self-esteem, less stress, and taking control of your life. The only person who can make you happier and more positive is you. Nobody else can change your life but you. Here are the five single most important changes to make in your everyday life that can change your outlook on life, and yourself.

1. Maintain a Healthy Diet

The best way to begin your transformation into a more positive person is to change your diet. What nourishes your body also nourishes your mind, and it is important to always maintain a healthy diet.

Foods that are loaded with sugars and sodium only drag your body down and make you feel sluggish, tired, and worn out. By replacing these foods with healthy fruits, vegetables, and whole grains, you will begin to feel the difference almost immediately. You will have more energy, and a much clearer mind. You will wake up feeling refreshed, and maintain that feeling throughout your day.

2. Implement an Exercise Routine

Just as nourishing your body with the proper foods will help you feel better, so too will exercise. However, you must ensure that you train your entire body, and each muscle.

In order to work out, try creating a fitness routine for yourself. It should be a combination of different workouts. Some examples include cardio, yoga, running, weights, and strength training. Exercising releases endorphins, which causes a natural high. You will feel your troubles melt away, and you will feel much happier with yourself. You should also exercise your mind, and keep it as sharp as possible.

Exercising your mind can help you cleanse your thoughts of stress and the worries of life, focusing instead on the task at hand. Exercising both your body and your mind also comes with a wealth of health benefits on top of helping you become a more positive person.

Exercise helps you decrease your risk for obesity, diabetes, heart disease, and many more serious illnesses and diseases. Working out your brain, on the other hand, has shown to help prevent degenerative brain diseases like Alzheimer's and dementia.

3. Think Positively

Thinking positively in order to be a more positive person may not make sense right away, as many will wonder if that isn't the whole point anyways. But thinking positively can play out in a variety of ways.

Every day, think of a mantra about yourself that you can repeat, willing yourself to believe it and internalize it. It could be anything, from "I am beautiful" to "I will get through today," anything that you think that you need to hear. Each person should have a different mantra that is unique to them, something that will give them the push that they need to better their own belief in themselves.

Your mantra may not even be about yourself. If you are facing a challenging task at work or in your personal life, make your mantra about that. "I can do this", or "I will be successful" are often powerful confidence boosters that are necessary to complete a task.

You should not feel silly about having a mantra. In fact, you should embrace it. Mantras are powerful tools of meditation and positive thinking.

4. Keep Good Company

Nothing can influence or change your thoughts like the company you are with. If you are always around someone who thinks negatively, and always looks to the worst rather than the best, it will eventually begin to affect the way that you think about the world around you.

Likewise, if you surround yourself with friends who are positive thinkers, and who try and see the good in the world, rather than the bad, you will start to think and feel the same way. Your friends are some of the largest influences in your life, and can greatly affect the way that you think and feel.

Friends can also help remove the stress and negativity in your life. Some friends who are negative thinkers may actually add more stress and cause you more problems in your life. Positive friends will help you relieve your stress and make it easier for you to let go of the negativity in your life.

5. Positive Visualization of Goals

In order to ensure that you are successful in your endeavors, you need to visualize them positively. If you had a big meeting at work, imagine that you nailed it, and it will help your mind think better. If you stop stressing about it, you will find that you have an easier time at the meetings. If you imagine that you will tank the meeting, then you will psych yourself out and cause more stress, and chances are that you will have a harder time at the meeting.

Never think of yourself as failure, as your brain will hold onto that and make you more nervous and stressed. Thinking that you will succeed will help you calm your mind and relax, making it easier to handle anything that gets thrown your way.

Why did I just give you the 5 keys to a positive personality? Well, you see, when you have a positive personality, there are so many benefits attached. Having a positive personality, for one, will help you achieve your goals and get over those tasks that may seem too difficult to complete. With a positive personality, you will be admired and trusted by those around you.

Personal Benefits

First, let me tell you about the personal benefits of a positive personality.
When you have a positive attitude toward performing a task that seems difficult, your positive

personality will push you toward achieving the goal you have set. On another note, being determined and courageous will help you succeed.

By being organized, you will be able to play out a successful outcome for your goals and projects. When it comes to those who have negative personality trains, they are known for being disorganized and have a tendency to procrastinate. This is certainly not what you want.

Social Benefits of a Positive Personality

Regardless of whether it is business or personal relationships, your attitude will determine how others choose to deal with you. If you show that you are an honest person that has a large amount of integrity, other people are more likely to trust you.

People tend to enjoy associating with individuals that they feel are reliable and responsible. If the other individual is fair-minded and understanding, they appreciate it.

Consumers, for example, want to purchase items from a sales person they know is honest. Employers would like to find workers that are reliable and people like to be friends with others they know they can trust and count on.

Obviously, if a person has a reputation for being uncaring, dishonest or unreliable, they won't be receiving the same considerations from someone with a good personality.

Think about it, if you had a choice between buying from someone who had a questionable reputation or buying from someone you knew for a fact was honest, you would probably pick the one that is honest, unless there are some other major factors that is influencing you.

Mind you, there are some people who seem to have a good character, but they may be deceptive – this is something you will have to watch out for. People often talk about romantic relationships that went downhill once they discovered who the other person was on the inside.

Cultural Benefits of Positive Personality

The attitude you have towards culture, religion or the rules of your government will determine how others that are in a group will view you. Often times, going against the rules can result in banishment or punishment.

If you follow the laws of your community, you will be more likely to benefit from it and will be considered a law-abiding citizen. On another note, breaking the laws could cause you to face time in jail. Even neighborhoods have loose rules that you should follow and following them will not only benefit you, but every other person in your neighborhood.

Point blank, if you follow the rules of your culture, you are going to benefit by feelings of belonging and are accepted by others. Breaking the rules will only bring about a feeling of disapproval.

In conclusion, by having good character, you will benefit. Your good personal character will help you along as you live out your life – it will help you achieve even the most difficult tasks and goals. Positive social character will help you become admired and trusted by others. Following the rules of your culture will give you the benefit of fitting in and being accepted by that group of people.

7: Psychology Tricks You Can Use to Help People

If you think that psychology is only meant to be used by people that hold a degree in that subject, you are already in for a big surprise! Psychology is not only a theoretical subject, but can be applied to person's everyday life. You will be surprised how much we use psychology already.

If you happen to be the type of person who likes to help other people, there are many simple, everyday psychology tricks that you can use - you may already be using them already. In order to better understand psychology and how to utilize this technique to be a better friend, sibling, son or daughter, co-worker, or just about anyone who is in need, continue reading below:

1. Understanding Others

How better to help another person, especially when they are going through a tough time or a personal crisis, than by being there for that person. Be their confidant, the person they can run to when they need someone to lean on.

What we generally think as kindness or empathy, in psychology terms it is known as EQ, or a person's Emotional Quotient. According to well-known psychologist, Daniel Goleman, EQ is probably more important than a person's IQ.

Personally, I think this is very true because what is your incredible mathematical or scientific skills going to do when your friend is in a crisis? You could probably invent something to make their lives easier but kidding aside, your loved one would probably appreciate it more if you could just try to understand them a little better and empathize in what they are going through.

But you may be wondering what you can do in order to increase your personal intelligence. Here are few tricks and tips that our might want to consider next time:

- Be conscious about your emotional reactions and reflect on whether these reactions are the appropriate to your friend's situation.

- Further reflect on your experiences through journal writing.

- And the most important, in my opinion and the best way you can easily empathize with a person is by trying to imagine yourself in that person's shoes. If you could walk a mile in that person's shoes (or at least imagine it), it will be easier to understand where they are coming from and you will figure out way to help them out.

Surprisingly, not many people have the ability to naturally empathize with others and it shouldn't be a surprise because all people have a tendency to be self-serving and selfish. However, the strategies mentioned above are the most helpful and yet simple ways you can help a person.

2. Communicating Well

Now that you have the listening skills down pat, you will also need to offer advice or give caring words to the person you are trying to help. Helping is so much more than just listening to their problems and then just giving them a gentle pat on the back. You also need to be willing to give advice (hopefully good ones) and encourage them. Being a good communicator is extremely important. I'm sure we've all been in a situation where we ended up saying the wrong thing to a person we were trying to help, right? Therefore, here are few tips to make sure that you end up saying the RIGHT things:

- Good eye contact. Believe it or not, eye contact is so important when trying to communicate your intentions. Words can seem hollow and empty sometimes, even if you are being entirely sincere. If you plan to appear sincere as well, you need to have good eye contact.

- Another way to become a better communicator without having to say anything first is by gauging the other person's body language and behavior. This is generally where people end up making a mistake when trying to encourage or give advice to the other person. Sometimes, we are so focused on trying to give advice that we completely disregard whether that person is in willing or in the mindset to hear what you have to say. That is why we need to start noticing the other person's body language and nonverbal behavior first.

- Now, we are in the position to actually do some verbal communicating. We have to make sure that our tone of voice is appropriate for the situation. Tone is very important in order to communicate your intentions with that person and to give them the feeling that you are genuinely willing to help them.

3. Decision-making

Usually, when a person comes to you for help or advice, they want someone to help them make a decision. Accurate decision-making can be hard especially when it involves doing this for another person.

What if you make the wrong decision for that person? Decision-making for yourself, when it is wrong can be very difficult for sure but at least you aren't necessarily hurting anyone else but yourself.

However, when trying to decide for someone else, oh boy, good luck if you do end up making the wrong decision for them! Hope your relationship with that person is still intact.

When it comes to making decisions, cognitive psychology has become a veritable gold mine. If you want to make good decisions for yourself and others from now on, you might want to consider these psychologically based strategies:

- Use the "six thinking hats" approach. Look at the situation from multiple perspectives, whether it is rational or logical sense, emotional sense, etc.

- Weigh the pros and cons. In order to make the best decisions possible, you really need to weigh the positive and the negative in whatever situation you or the person you are helping is in. This also gives you a more thorough and overall look at the entire situation. I personally, really like making the list of pros and cons when I need to make a big decision.

You can employ these psychology tricks in order to

help others and maybe yourself in our daily, everyday lives.

Conclusion

In the end, I enjoyed helping you learn how to help others who have emotional problems. Remember, helping those who are dealing with emotional problems isn't going to be an easy road – it may take a lot of work, but in the end, when you finally see a smile on their face, you will realize just how happy it made you in return. Trust me, there's nothing better in this world than seeing a smile upon someone's face – a smile YOU put there. This life is full of twists and turns, you never really know what is at the end of the road. Remember to take one step at a time and when you see another person going through an emotional time in their life, be there to offer guidance and show them that you care.

Hopefully, now you have a better understanding of psychology how you use the techniques in this book to help other people!

May I ask a small favor from you? If you can find the time, can you please leave an honest review for this book? Whether it is good or bad, I would really appreciate it! I am always striving to improve my book.

Thank You!

www.ingramcontent.com/pod-product-compliance
Lightning Source LLC
Chambersburg PA
CBHW071224280526
45787CB00002B/792